PEACE IS THIS MOMENT

BREATHE AS A FREE PERSON

You can practice freedom every moment of your daily life. Every step you take can help you reclaim your freedom. Every breath you take can help you develop and cultivate your freedom. When you eat, eat as a free person. When you walk, walk as a free person. When you breathe, breathe as a free person. This is possible anywhere.

WHEN MINDFULNESS SHINES

Thanks
to the sun, plants can
grow. There are other conditions
for the growth of plants, like rain and
soil, but the sun is the primary source of energy
for living things. When mindfulness arises, it can
transform other mental formations. Mindfulness is
like the sun. It only has to shine its light to do its work.

HAPPINESS
IS MADE
OF THESE
MOMENTS

Happiness is made of moments of mindfulness
and concentration. When you're happy, when you have enough
mindfulness and concentration, you feel good within yourself,
and then you can help other living beings.

THIS
IS IT

The opportunity you have been waiting for
is right here in the present moment.
Each breath is an opportunity for you
to go back to the now, to stop
your endless wandering.

The day you've been waiting for is today;
the moment you've been waiting for
is this very moment.

I
HEAR
ALREADY

Anything that can help you wake up has buddha nature.
When I'm alone and a bird calls me, I return to myself.
I breathe and smile, and sometimes it calls me once more.
I smile and I say to the bird, "I hear already."

A LIBERATING SMILE

You may think a smile is nothing, but it's a lot.
With a true smile, you make all the generations of ancestors in
you smile. It is liberation; it is transformation.
Every mindful in-breath, every mindful out-breath,
every peaceful step, every smile is an act of liberation.

PEACE
IS HERE

Peace can exist only in the present moment.
It's ridiculous to say, "Wait until I finish this, then I will be free
to live in peace." What is "this"? A diploma, a job, a house, the
payment of a debt? If you think that way, peace will never come.
If you truly want to be at peace,
you must be at peace right now.

OUR
IDEA OF
HAPPINESS

Each of us is caught in an idea of happiness.
We believe we'll be truly happy only when certain conditions
are fulfilled. We don't realize that this idea is an obstacle to our
true happiness. If we can release our idea of happiness,
true happiness is born in us right away.

Why do we commit ourselves to only one idea of happiness?
If we let go of that idea, happiness will come to us
from every direction.

BECOME LIKE A CHILD

Children have more capacity to be in the here and now than adults. They don't think too much about the future. They don't create a lot of projects like we do, and they aren't caught up in the past. So learning to be more like children is a good practice.

STEP
IN THE
DIRECTION
OF LIFE

There is no need for us to struggle to arrive somewhere else.
We know our final destination is the cemetery.
Why are we in a hurry to get there?
Why not step in the direction of life,
which is in the present moment?

THERE IS AWAKENING

When we breathe in and bring our mind back to our body, when we're truly present—body and mind united—there is awakening. We know we're alive; we're present, and life is there for us to live.

Awakening isn't something very far away. We only need to bring our mind back to our body and be truly here in the present moment.

ENJOY
SITTING
HERE

If you allow your body to sit in a relaxing, peaceful way,
it calms your body and mind.

Effortlessness is the key to success.

Sitting like this allows you to enjoy your in-breath and
out-breath, to enjoy sitting here, to enjoy being alive.

BE
YOURSELF

We tend to think we have to do something
to heal ourselves. But sitting with mindfulness and concentration
is already enough. Just sit quietly and be yourself. Don't strive;
relaxation will come. When you're completely relaxed,
healing will take place on its own.

DE-
COM-
PART-
MENT-
ALIZING
OUR LIVES

If a doctor gives you an injection, your whole body benefits, not only your arm. If you practice sitting meditation one hour a day, that hour should benefit all twenty-four hours. One smile, one breath should be for the benefit of the whole day, not just that moment. We must practice in a way that removes the barrier between practice and non-practice.

LIKE A DREAM

Too often we're carried along by the energy of the people around us, by circumstances, or by our own thoughts.

Ask yourself, "What have I done with my life over the past few years?" If you have not practiced stopping, the years will seem to have gone by like a dream. Without stopping and looking deeply, we can't really live our lives.

WHY WAIT TO BE HAPPY?

Many people in our society aren't happy, even though the conditions for their happiness already exist. Their habit energy is always pushing them ahead, preventing them from being happy in the here and now. But with a little bit of training, we can all learn to recognize this energy every time it comes up. Why wait to be happy?

LOOKING AT A LOTUS FLOWER, SEEING THE MUD

There is a beautiful flower called a lotus that grows from the mud at the bottom of a pond and blooms on the surface. When we look into a lotus flower, we see the mud it grows in. Happiness is a kind of lotus—without the element of suffering, you cannot make happiness. Because there is mud, there can be a lotus.

BATHING IN THE LIGHT OF MINDFULNESS

If we were wounded as a young child, the seeds of suffering we received
are still with us today. The way we relate to life in the present
moment is partly based on these seeds of suffering, but because
we have not bathed them in the light of mindfulness,
we aren't aware of them. Recognition alone will
cause them to lose some of their
power over us.

NOTHING CAN LIVE WITHOUT FOOD

Looking deeply into our suffering, we can see the many causes and conditions that have brought it about. We can also see what feeds that suffering, what we continue to bring into our body and mind that keep our suffering alive. Nothing can live without food. When we've seen what feeds our suffering, we can decide to stop ingesting it.

STOP
TO LIVE
DEEPLY

We can practice concentration and looking deeply during all the activities of our daily life. Even while walking, we can practice stopping. We can walk in a way that doesn't make arriving the only goal. We can walk to enjoy each step. If we practice stopping while sweeping the floor, washing the dishes, or taking a shower, we live deeply. Stopping helps us live authentically.

FOOT
PRINTS
ON THE
EARTH

We walk all the time, but usually it's more like running. When we walk
in this way, we print anxiety and sorrow on the earth.
Every one of us can walk in a way that leaves only
peace and serenity imprinted on the earth.
When we can take one step peacefully,
happily, we support the cause of
peace and happiness for
all humankind.

MAINTAINING OUR FLOWERNESS

Just by breathing in and out and smiling, we offer a flower.
A flower doesn't have to do anything to be of service; it only has to
be a flower. That is enough. Being truly present is enough to make the
whole world rejoice. So please practice breathing in and out and
recover your flowerness. You do it for all of us.

GENERATING JOY

The practice of mindfulness is an art. We train ourselves to be able to generate a feeling of joy and happiness at any time, no matter what the situation. We learn to see that mindfulness is a source of happiness because it helps us to be in touch with the many wonders of life.

LIGHT UP THE LAMP OF HAPPINESS

When we learn to generate a feeling of happiness, we create
happiness both for ourselves and for other people.
It is contagious. By cultivating happiness, we
remind people around us to be happy.
We remind them that they are in
a wonderful world where the
wonders of life are available
to them, and that makes
them happy.

We light up the lamp of happiness in them.

SKILLFUL WEAVING

We have to touch both the healthy and the ailing parts of our body and consciousness to touch the truth. The truth will help us be happy and joyful. We have to embrace our unhealthy parts tenderly and mindfully, weaving them into the fabric of our otherwise healthy bodies and minds.

SMILE TO
YOURSELF

There are times when your joy makes you smile. There are also times when a smile causes relaxation, calm, and joy. I don't wait until there's joy in me to smile; joy will come later. Sometimes when I'm alone in my room, I practice smiling to myself. I do this to be kind to myself, to take good care of myself, to love myself. I know that if I cannot take care of myself, I cannot take care of anyone else.

LIVING
IN THE
SPIRIT OF
GRATITUDE

Just by practicing gratitude, we can find happiness.
We must be grateful to our ancestors, our parents, our teachers,
our friends, the earth, the sky, the trees, the grass, the animals,
the soil, the stones. Looking at the sunlight or at the forest,
we feel gratitude. Looking at our breakfast, we feel gratitude.
When we live in the spirit of gratitude, there will be much
happiness in our life.

HOW TO LIVE

There are always enough
internal and external conditions
to make us happy in the present
moment. This isn't to deny
that there are also elements of
suffering in us and around us.
But the elements of suffering
don't remove the elements of
happiness. If we touch only the
elements of suffering, we aren't
really living.

HAPPINESS
IS THE
WAY

There is no way to happiness; happiness is the way.

Happiness should be found in every moment of your daily life,

not at the end of the road. Life is now, in every second, in every

moment. Peace is every step; happiness is every step.

It's so clear and simple.

ELEGANT
SILENCE

You don't need to talk to communicate. If you sit and radiate
peace, stability, and joy, you offer something very precious to
the other person. If the other person is truly present and
sitting with solidity and peace, you can receive a lot
of energy from them. True communication is
possible in silence. Silence can be
very elegant.

THE
CAPACITY
TO
TAKE CARE

Love is the capacity to take care, protect, and nourish.
If you can't generate that kind of energy toward yourself, it's very
difficult to take care of another person.

THE ART OF MAKING ONE PERSON HAPPY

By learning the art of
making one person happy,
you learn to express your love
for the whole of humanity
and all beings.

MEDITATION
IN DAILY
LIFE

If you're aware of what is going on, you can see problems
as they unfold, and you can help prevent many of them.
When things explode, it's too late. How we deal with
our daily lives is the most important question.
How we deal with our feelings, our speaking,
and ordinary things every day is meditation.
We must learn to apply meditation
in our daily lives.

NON-
ACTION

Sometimes if we don't do anything,
we help more than if we do a lot.
We call that non-action. It's like a calm
person on a small boat in a storm:
that person doesn't have to
do much—just be themselves—
and the situation can change.

REAL
HAPPINESS

Our life will be filled with happiness if we can help others around us. But if we spend our whole life building up our name and our fortune, we cannot find happiness. We might have a lot of money, a big house, and a luxurious car, but that's not real happiness. We can only taste real happiness when we can help others.

PEACE
BEGINS
WITH
ME

Any step we take in mindfulness that brings us a little more solidity, freedom, and joy also benefits society. Don't think what you do to yourself doesn't affect the rest of society and the world. Peace and freedom always begin with our own practice. If peace is in you, peace becomes possible everywhere in the cosmos.

THAT IS
PEACE

Are we doing anything to help end violence? If we allow ourselves to be overwhelmed by feelings of anger and despair, we won't be able to help. We may even add fuel to the situation, increase its intensity, and make it last longer. The question is whether we can do something for peace—be something for peace—right in the present moment.

COLLECTIVE KARMA

We must be aware that we're always in the process of creating our environment with our thoughts, words, and actions. In this way, we contribute to creating our collective environment, our society. If society is full of violence, fear, and hate, it's partly our collective karma. We have allowed things to become this way. With awakening, enlightenment, and mindfulness, we can change things.

YOU HAVE TO REALLY WANT IT

To be free means you're no longer the victim of fear, worries, anger, or craving. Maybe you want freedom, but you don't want it enough. You have other desires that get in the way, such as wanting a bigger house or a better car. Those little desires distract you from your most noble desire. If you want to realize your deep desire, you have to really want it.

KNOW
THE
LIMIT

We must know the limit, we must know
how much is enough. This is the antidote for wanting
more and more: you know what is sufficient,
what is enough for you.

UNDISTURBED BY THE EBB AND FLOW OF LIFE

If we see someone who isn't disturbed by the ebb and flow of life, not enmeshed in afflictions, that person has freedom; that person is solid. When we also master this quality, our worldly afflictions dissolve, and we become indestructible—completely at peace. We do this by practicing happiness in the present moment.

THE MIRACLE IS TO WALK ON EARTH

Our true home is the present moment—to live in the present moment is a miracle. The miracle isn't to walk on water. The miracle is to walk on the green earth in the present moment, to appreciate the peace and beauty available now.

NO NEED FOR IMPROVEMENT

We don't need to criticize ourselves or others for
moments of forgetfulness. We don't even need to try
to improve ourselves. All we need is to be in the moment.
The next one will be quite different.
The present moment has all we need.

YOU
ALREADY
ARE WHAT
YOU WANT
TO BE

When we work too hard at anything, whether it's business or enlightenment, then we can't see the wonders of life inside and around us. You already are what you want to be. There is nothing to attain. Stop. Don't do anything.

A CONTINUOUSLY FLOWING STREAM

Looking into your body, you will
discover that you aren't a separate self,
cut off from everything else, but a
continuously flowing stream—
the stream of life itself.

HEALING
WITH
THE EARTH

The earth is filled with love and patience.
Walking mindfully on the earth, we're nourished by the trees,
the bushes, the flowers, and the sunshine. Whether the earth is
beautiful, fresh, and green or arid and parched depends on
our way of walking. Please touch the earth in mindfulness,
with joy and concentration. The earth will heal you,
and you will heal the earth.

ABANDONING OUR VIEWS

In Zen, knowledge is regarded as an obstacle to understanding, like a block of ice that obstructs water from flowing. It's said that if we take one thing to be the truth and cling to it, then even if truth itself knocks at our door, we won't open it. For things to reveal themselves to us, we need to be ready to abandon our views about them.

ANY SUBJECT CAN BRING ABOUT AWAKENING

Any subject can bring about awakening
if it's sown deeply into the ground of your being.

But if it's only entrusted to your intellect,
it's unlikely to bear fruit.

REPAIRING THE PAST

We think the past is gone and the future is not yet here. But if we look deeply, we see that the past exists in the guise of the present because the present is made from the past. If we touch the present moment deeply, we also touch the past and have the power to repair it. We don't have to bear our wounds forever.

MAKE YOUR HEART LIKE THE RIVER

If you stir a handful of salt into a bowl of water, the water becomes too salty to drink. But if you pour that salt water into a river, the river is too large to be affected. If your heart is spacious like the river, you won't suffer because of small problems.

SPIRITUALITY IS A PRACTICE

Spirituality isn't just belief in a teaching; it's a practice.
Practice always brings relief and transformation.
Everyone's life needs a spiritual dimension.
With our practice, we can deal with
whatever we encounter
in our daily life.

A RIVER OF UNDER-STANDING

When we decide to live our lives with love and awakening, we enter a flowing river of understanding and compassion. That river has no beginning and no end. It contains our community, our ancestors, and future generations. I invite all of us, together as one, to relax and be carried by this river, to let it take us where we want to go.

THICH NHAT HANH (1926–2022) is one of
the most influential spiritual leaders in the world today
and a pioneer in bringing Buddhism to the West.

Parallax Press is the publishing division of
Plum Village Community of Engaged Buddhism, Inc.
Copyright © 2025 by Plum Village Community of Engaged Buddhism, Inc.
Printed in the United States of America on FSC ® certified acid-free paper
All rights reserved | ISBN 9780938077909
Cover and text design by Katie Eberle
Parallax Press's authorized representative in the EEA is
SARL Boutique La Bambouseraie Point UH,
Le Pey, 24240 Thénac, France
Email: europe@parallax.org

2 04